THE CHALICE OF ECSTASY

BEING
A MAGICAL AND QABALISTIC
INTERPRETATION OF THE DRAMA OF
PARZIVAL

BY
A COMPANION OF THE HOLY GRAIL
SOMETIMES CALLED
FRATER ACHAD

Dedicated to my Beloved Friend and Companion
FRATER AD ALTA
Who passed from our view into
THE GREAT HERE AND NOW
November 29th, 1918
exactly four years prior to the completion of this essay.

I

INTRODUCTION

The collective tradition of mankind is endowed with a relative infallibility, and when rightly interpreted, must represent the largest truth, the most perfect beauty and the purest goodness known on earth. This transcendental truth and goodness and beauty represents the divine substratum of human nature, the ideal humanity which lies above and behind the aberrations of individuals, races and periods. It is not subjected, as are the latter, to Time and Circumstance or to the limitations from which the appearance of error, evil and deformity seem to spring.

The Legend of Parzival is not subject to Time or Circumstance; it represents a glimpse of the Eternal Reality, the Everpresent Here and Now. The circumstances of its enactment and the place wherein the festival is beheld, need not be sought outside the Human Heart that has learned to beat in time and tune with the Soul of the World. All who are born of "Heart's Affliction" must eventually find their way to that spot where they "Scarcely move, yet swiftly seem to run" and having become one with "The Way, The Truth and The Life" they will discover that the shifting scenes of the world they had thought to be so real, will pass by them as a pageant until the Vision of the Grail Itself is presented to their pure Understanding.

It is in the hope of awakening some spark of the smouldering fire of this inner consciousness in the hearts of those who may read these lines - not having previously understood the Legend - and from that spark enkindling a great fire that will burn up the veils which hide man from Himself - from God - that I have dared to add these fragments to the great mass of Grail Literature already given to the world.

And to those who are slumbering contentedly, wrapped round with the delusion and dreams of this illusory like, I cry with Gurnemanz:

Hey! Ho! Wood-keepers twain! Sleep-keepers I deem ye! At least be moving with the morning! Hear ye the call? Now thank the Lord That ye are called in time to hear it.

Point I.
THE COMING OF PARZIVAL

"By pity 'lightened The guileless Fool - Wait for him, My chosen tool."

It is not my intention to set forth the complete Argument of the Great Musical-Drama of "Parsifal" derived from the ancient legend of Parzival by Richard Wagner, to whom be all praise and honour.

Those who have not had the privilege of witnessing this festival-play, or even of reading a good translation of the Libretto, should avail themselves of the help that a study of the latter will give them before expecting to gain a thorough grasp of the interpretation herein set forth. [1]

I shall also suppose that the student has some slight knowledge of The Mystic Path and of The Holy Qabalah, [2] although I shall endeavor to make the points dealt with as comprehensive as possible to the uninitiated enquirer who is prepared to "wake and hearken to the Call".

The Music of Wagner I cannot give you, nor shall I even attempt an interpretation of that which, in the Opera, helps so much toward the opening of those channels of consciousness whereby we may eventually receive some comprehensive of the Music of the Spheres.

Fortunately this is not entirely necessary, for the true Path leads to a point when each individual may feel himself to be a highly-strung musical instrument whose Will runs over the strings causing complete and harmonious vibrations in his own being, which will then seem to give forth an unformulated but delightful melody.

What is the Keynote of Parzival?
ECSTASY!

And what is Ecstasy? It has been well described by one known to us as Frater Perdurabo, and I shall quote his own words:

"There is a land of pure delight, Where saints immortal reign."

"So used some of us to sing in childhood, and we used to think of that land as far away, farther even than death that in those days seemed so far.

"But I know this now: that land is not so far as my flesh is from my bones! it is Here and Now.

"If there is one cloud in this tranquil azure, it is this thought: that conscious beings exist who are not thus infinitely happy, masters of ecstasy.

"What is the path to this immortal land? To the Oriental, meditation offers the best path. To the Western, there is no road better than ceremonial. For ecstasy is caused by the sudden combination of two ideas, just as oxygen and hydrogen unite explosively.

"But this religious ecstasy takes place in the highest centres of the human organism; it is the soul itself that is united to its God; and for this reason the rapture is more overpowering, the joy more lasting, and the resultant energy more pure and splendid than in aught earthly.

"In ritual therefore, we seek continually to unite the mind to some pure idea by an act of will. This we do again and again, more and more passionately, with more and more determination, until at last the mind accepts the domination of the will, and rushes of its own accord toward the desired object. This surrender of the mind to its Lord gives the holy ecstasy we seek."

Here we have one of the most important keys to the interpretation of the Drama of Parzival, and also an indication of the result which Wagner desired to produce upon the minds of his audience.

Unless the Play is properly staged, and the parts taken by those who themselves understand at least something of the "Way of Holiness", this effect is not made upon the consciousness of the onlookers. This is doubtless one the reasons why Wagner made arrangements that this Work should only be produced at Bayreuth in a proper setting and under right conditions, for it represents the summit of his Magical Mountain of which the base was the Ring. He called it a Stage-Consecrating Festival, and its effects were intended to exert their influence upon the Drama of Life itself.

We will pass over the early part of the opening Scene with its introduction of Gurnemanz, Kundry, and Amfortas, and concentrate our attention on the entry of Parzival; heralded by the falling of a Swan brought down by his own weapon.

What is this Swan?

Ecstasy!

How do I know? Never mind, let me quote once again from one who is the Master thereof:

THE SWAN

"There is a Swan whose name is Ecstasy; it wingeth from the deserts of the North; it wingeth through the blue; it wingeth over the fields of rice; at its coming they push forth the green. In all the Universe this Swan alone in motionless; it seems to move, as the Sun seems to move; such is the weakness of our sight. O fool! criest thou? Amen. Motion is relative: there is Nothing that is still. Against this Swan I shot an arrow; the white breast poured forth blood. Men smote me; then perceiving that I was a Pure Fool, they let me pass. Thus and not otherwise I came to the Temple of the Grail."

Thus did Parzival bring down Ecstasy to Earth, although the King - Amfortas - and his Knights had "esteemed it a happy token, when o'er the lake it circled aloft".

What is this lake? When calm and unruffled, brooded over by the Swan of Ecstasy, it is the human mind trained by the proper methods to Right Contemplation. For only when the mind is still may the Sun of the true Self be seen reflected in its depths. From that it is but one step to the attainment of Right Ecstasy when the Sun plunges into the depths of the Mind and the whole being is aflame with the Sacred Fire of the Holy Spirit.

Parzival had aimed high; he had hit the mark of his Aspiration, little though his action was at first understood. Yet his Folly saved him, as he in turn saved others.

When questioned as to his action he answered "I knew not 'twas wrong" although he flung away weapon, having no further use for it in that form.

What was his weapon? The Bow of Promise and the Arrow of Pure Aspiration. But he had aspired, he had hit the mark and the promise had been to a certain extent fulfilled.

The Qabalist will at once recognise the "Path of Samech or Sagittarius the Archer on the 'Tree of Life.'" This is the Path of the Arrow that cleaves the Rainbow, leading directly from Yesod - The Foundation - to Tiphareth the Sphere of the Sun, Beauty and Harmony, or the Human Heart wherein the Mysteries of the Rosy Cross and of the Holy Grail are first - if dimly - perceived.

To what other use had Parzival - son of Herat's Affliction - previously put his weapon? He had shot at all that flies. He had shot at the Eagle, the bird that fears not to gaze upon the very Sun itself.

What does this eagle mean and what does it foreshadow? ECSTASY!

For it is written: "The Eagle is that Might of Love which is the Key of Magick, uplifting the Body and its appurtenance unto High Ecstasy upon his Wings."

This Eagle is known to Occultists as one of the Four Cherubic Beasts and he represents one of the Four Powers of the Sphinx. Likewise he is attributed by Eliphas Levi to Azoth, the formula of the Alpha and Omega, the First and Last.

It was by the right use of this Might of Love that Parzival succeeded where others had failed. For again it is written in Liber Aleph:

"Consider Love. Here is a force destructive and corrupting whereby have many men been lost: witness all History. Yet without love man were not man.

"We see Amfortas, who yielded himself to a seduction, wounded beyond healing; Klingsor, who withdrew himself from a like danger , cast out forever from the Mountain of Salvation, and Parzival who yielded not, able to exercise the true Power of Love and thereby to perform the Miracle of Redemption."

But though we are now nearing that realm wherein "Time and Space are One" we must not allow ourselves to be rushed forward too rapidly.

There were many things that Parzival did not know, or which he professed not to know when questioned. He did now as yet know he True Name - the Word of His Being - though he had in the past been called by many names. Some things he knew and remembered clearly; there was one thing he desired to know and to understand.

What is the Grail!

To which Gurnemanz very properly replies:

I may not say: But if to serve it thou be bidden, Knowledge of it will not be hidden.- And lo!- Methinks I know thee now indeed; No earthly road to it doth lead, By no one can it be detected Who by itself is not elected.

To which Parzival, without further questioning, replies:

I scarcely move, Yet I swiftly seem to run.

And Gurnemanz:

My son, thou seest Here SPACE and TIME are ONE.

Now, in truth, have we come to the beginning of the True Path which in the clear Light is one with the end thereof.

What says Blavatsky in "The Voice of the Silence"? "Bestride the Bird of Life if thou wouldst know!"

And this Bird - this Swan - so seeming dead until its Powers be known? Some have compared it to the Sacred Word, the Great Word AUM. For it is written: "AUM is the hieroglyph of the Eternal. A the beginning sound, U its middle and M its end, together forming a single Word or Trinity, indicating that the Real must be regarded as of this three-fold nature. Birth, Life and Death, not successive, but one."

The Illusory nature of Time and Space, which are but modes of our finite mind, has been made very clear by Sidney Klein in his excellent book "Science and the Infinite," but this is no new

9

idea. The attainment of Ecstasy has proved to Initiates of every land that there is a state of consciousness wherein both time and space are blotted out - at least temporarily - and at the same moment the limitations of the "personal ego" no longer oppress us. In that Holy Book known as Liber LXV- Chapter II, Verses 17-25, we read:

"17. Also the Holy One came upon me, and I beheld a white swan floating in the blue.

18. Between its wings I sate, and the aeons fled away.

19. Then the swan flew and dived and soared, yet no whither we went.

20. A little crazy boy that rode with me spake unto the swan and said:

21. Who art thou that doth float and fly and dive and soar in the inane? Behold, these many aeons have passed; whence camest thou? Whither wilt thou go?

22. And laughing I chid him saying: No whence! No wither!

23. The swan being silent, he answered: Then if with no goal, why this eternal journey?

24. And I laid my head against the Head of the Swan, and laughed, saying: Is there not joy ineffable in this aimless winging? Is there not weariness and impatience for who would attain to some goal?

25. And the swan was ever silent. Ah, but we floated in the infinite Abyss. Joy! Joy! White swan bear thou ever me up between thy wings."

But there was much that Parzival must do before taking his ease thus: he had a mission to accomplish, on earth, though as yet he knew not.

By the use of these examples, we may begin to comprehend what happens next. A new "movement without motion" on the part of Parzival and Gurnemanz is now symbolized by the SCENERY in the Drama shifting, at first almost imperceptibly, from Left to Right. The forest - in which the First Scene had taken place - disappears; a door opens in the rocky cliffs and conceals the two; they are then seen again in sloping passages which they appear to ascend. At last they arrive at a mighty hall, which loses itself overhead in a high vaulted dome, down from which the light streams in. From the heights above the dome comes the increasing sound of chimes.

Again we may find a very direct correspondence in the Eastern Teachings as propounded by Madame Blavatsky in "The Voice of Silence." She writes: "Thou canst travel on that Path until thou hast become the Path itself."

Further in Liber CCCXXXIII by Frater Perdurabo we read:

"O thou that settest out upon the Path, false is the Phantom that thou seekest. When thou hast it thou shalt know all bitterness, thy teeth fixed in the Sodom-Apple. Thus hast thou been lured along That Path, whose terror else had driven thee far away. O thou that stridest upon the middle of The Path, no phantoms mock thee. For the stride's sake thou stridest. Thus art thou lured along That Path whose fascination else had driven thee far away.

"O thou that drawest toward the End of The Path, effort is no more. Faster and faster dost thou fall; thy weariness is changed into Ineffable Rest. For there is no Thou upon that Path: thou hast become The Way."

And each must learn to travel this Path, each must overcome his own obstacles, unmask his own illusions. Yet there is always the possibility that others may help us do this and, as in the case of Parzival led by Gurnemanz who travelled that Way before, we may be guided in the true Path and taught to avoid the many false byways that may tempt us in our search for the Temple of the Holy Grail. In fact, if our training has been right and our aspiration remains pure, we must inevitably arrive at the end of that Road; often we may seem to do so in the twinkling of an eye, and when we least expect it.

We should remember that every point of this Drama is highly symbolic. The student may place his own interpretation on that passage which opens into the Temple of the Grail. On arrival therein we cannot do better than listen to the advice of

Gurnemanz to Parzival, who meanwhile stands spellbound with Wonder at what he beholds:

Now give good head, and let me see, If thou'rt a Fool and pure, What wisdom thou presently canst secure.

And this WISDOM Parzival does in due course secure, but not until he has undergone many trials. For WISDOM is the HOLY SPEAR itself, long lost to the Knights of the Grail but eventually recovered by The Pure Fool.

Meanwhile, during the Feast of the Grail, Parzival stands still and spellbound like a rude clod. He sees the CUP of the Grail uncovered, he witnesses the ceremony of the Companions of the Grail, and he attains a certain interior UNDERSTANDING which transcends knowledge. For the CUP is the UNDERSTANDING, though in this instance it was divorced from the WILL or WISDOM, the Holy Spear which alone is capable of enlightening it perfectly.

A word may now be said regarding the nature of "The Pure Fool"; and since this Ritual is one for all time, we shall go back before the Christian Era (to which the Grail Mystery is usually particularly attributed) back to Ancient China where the testimony of that Holy Sage Lao Tze gives us no uncertain clue. The Way of the Tao - Wu Wei - the accomplishment of all things by doing Nothing, is precisely similar to the "Path" we have been describing. Lao Tze says:

"The multitude of men look satisfied and pleased as if enjoying a full banquet, as if mounted on a tower in spring. I alone seem listless and still, my desires having as yet given no indication of their presence. I am like an infant which has not yet smiled. I look dejected and forlorn, as I had no home to go to. The multitude of men all have enough and to spare. I alone seem to have lost everything. My mind is that of a stupid man; I am in a state of chaos. Ordinary men look bright and intelligent, while I alone seem to be benighted. They look full of discrimination, while I alone am dull and confused. I seem to be carried about as on a sea, drifting as if I had nowhere to rest. All men have their spheres of action, while I alone seem dull and incapable, like a rude borderer. Thus I ALONE AM DIFFERENT from other men, but I value the Nursing-Mother (The Great Tao)."

So we see this Fool is not the ordinary sort of foolish and besotted person to which the form is usually applied. In his Foolishness we find his difference from his fellows; for in sooth it is the Divine Madness of Ecstasy which redeems from all pain. It is "That which remains" after the sorrows and shadows that pass and are done, have left our being. Then Existence is recognized to be Pure Joy. But Understanding without Wisdom is Pure Darkness, and in this state is Parzival discovered by Gurnemanz at the end of the Ceremony. This is a darkness even Guernemanz is unable to comprehend, for he says:

Why standest thou there? Wist thou what thou sawest?

And Parzival, shaking his head slightly, he continues:

Thou art then nothing but a Fool!

And pushing Parzival through a small door he cries angrily:

Come away, on thy road the gone And put my rede to use: Leave all our swans for the future alone And seek thyself a gander, a goose.

And so it came about that Parzival set out alone upon his Holy Quest.

Point II
THE TEMPTING OF PARZIVAL

"For pure will, unassuaged of purpose, delivered from the lust of result, is every way perfect." Liber Al. vel. Legis

The last Scene of the First Act of this Drama will have enabled us to see something of the nature of the "Heart" or Temple of the Knights of the Grail. We are next transported to the "Keep" of Klingsor's Castle, there to obtain a glimpse of the Heart of a Black Magician. Klingsor represents one who has "shut himself up", who desires to keep his personality and while retaining possession of the SPEAR or Divine Will to make use of it, if possible for his own personal ends.

Man is given a certain freedom of will in order that he may thereby develop the sense of Freedom and so willingly ally himself with the Divine Will or True Purpose of his Being. Should he make the mistake of attempting to reverse the process, turning the Divine Will to merely personal ends, he must inevitably fall. He thereby cuts himself off from the Universal Current and is slowly but surely disintegrated until he is finally lost in the Abyss.

For a time, however, as in the case of Klingsor, he may seem to exercise an illusionary power by taking advantage of the delusions of others. For he plays upon their emotional natures, which tend if uncontrolled to befog the mind thus preventing the True Sun of Being from illuminating their Path.

Self-damned, the one desire of such a being is to cause the utter ruin and downfall of others in order that the terrible loneliness which he - if dimly - realizes to be his fate, may be assuaged by the presence of his victims.

Klingsor, however, still hopes to capture the Holy CUP itself - which has remained in the possession of the Knights of the Grail - for this is the Cup of UNDERSTANDING whereby he may discover a way to reverse this fate and to make use of its contents, the Divine Substance which is capable of infinite transformation when united with the Spear or WILL.

Even without this perfect means of transmutation, he has still obtained a certain power over Astral Matter, which being of a very plastic nature is capable of transformation into images alluring or terrible according to the effect to be produced upon his victims.

The Aspirant has been warned of the illusory nature of the Astral Plane in "The Voice of Silence" which contains instructions for those ignorant of the dangers of the lower Siddhi (magical powers). We shall refer to these instructions again in the proper place.

Meanwhile, as the Act opens, we discover Klingsor seated before his magic mirror in the Keep of his Castle. He is surrounded with the instruments of his art, which are as complex as the true weapons are simple.

He is evidently aware of the coming of Parzival - the Guileless Fool - and he realizes that here is a menace to his power, since that power depends upon beguilement. The question before him is whether this Fool is really too Pure to be tempted by the subtle blandishments of his magic art.

Kundry - Woman - capable alike of raising man to the heights or dragging him to the very depths, is the best instrument to his hand. She - the Animal Soul of the World - while directed by the lower will or intellect - has within her not alone the possibilities of redemption, but of taking her rightful place upon the Throne of the Mother if brought to Understanding the Higher Will and Wisdom of the Father of All.

On the other hand if under the influence of the lower will she is allowed to seduce man from his aspiration, do that he fails to discover his True Will (which is one with Destiny and the Will of God and which alone can direct him in his proper course) she ruins him and at the same time loses her own chance of redemption. He is then doomed to wander in paths of illusion having no comprehension of the true Purpose of his Being or hers.

Klingsor exercises a mighty power over Kundry whenever she allows herself to fall asleep, though much of her time during waking hours is devoted to the service of the Knights of the Grail. Many of these she has injured while under the spell of Klingsor. She often desires to make amends but her heart is torn between this form of activity and desire for case.

Whenever she sinks back into the sloth of Ignorance, or what the Hindus term the Tamas Guna, she is subject to the art of Klingsor for he is the maker of Illusion through Learning or the Powers of the mind, the principle known as Rajas. By means of this mental power many false uses may be devised for the Love nature, which when wrongly used becomes destructive instead of Creative and constructive.

Parzival - The Pure Fool - is in that condition mentioned by Lao Tze "His desires having as yet given no indication of their presence." The crucial test is whether when they are aroused for the first time he will use them rightly or wrongly. Therein both Amfortas and Klingsor had failed, though in different ways. Now comes a third candidate in the form of Parzival and Klingsor fears greatly for the continuance of his own power.

He knows that even Kundry will be redeemed should Parzival, by rejecting her advances, and refusing to accept aught but the highest, cause her at last to Understand and so become released from Klingsor's illusory powers.

Klingsor first lights incense, which in true magick is a symbol of the aspiration of the lower towards the higher. But there is no Lamp above the altar, and the Lamp symbolizes the Higher Aspiration to draw up and unite the lower with itself. The incense alone produces nothing but the smoky clouds which represent the Astral Plane, and this plane being particularly attributed to the Desires and Emotions is the one most suited to the work Klingsor wishes Kundry to perform. It is her Astral body over which he has the most influence.

His call to her is worthy of notice:

Arise! Draw near me! The Master calls thee, nameless woman: She-Lucifer! Rose of Hades! Herodias wert thou. And what else? Gundryggia there, Kundry here! Approach! Approach then, Kundry! Unto thy Master appear!

And in the incense smoke now appears the figure of Kundry - her Astral form - half-obedient, half rebellious to the will of Klingsor.

The term "Rose of Hades" should be noticed here, for in a certain sense Kundry is that same Rose which is to be found in connection with the Cross in the Rosy Cross Ceremonies. The Cross of Suffering may be looked upon as represented by Amfortas - as can be shown Qabalistically - and the wound at his breast is caused by the Rose, Kundry. The Spear and Cup convey the same Symbolism but on a Higher Plane.

Meanwhile Kundry gradually comes under the spell of Klingsor, who orders her to use all her wiles to ensnare the approaching and victorious Parzival; "Whom sheerest Folly shields."

Klingsor, while admitting that he cannot hold Kundry, claims that he can force her to his will:

"Because against me Thine own power cannot move"

Kundry, laughing harshly, makes this strange reply:

Ha Ha! Art thou chaste!

This remark causes Klingsor to sink into gloomy brooding. He recalls how he, too, had once sought the holier life and the service of the Grail. But, unlike Amfortas who had succumbed to seduction, he, thinking to avoid a like fate had used his will to attempt something against Nature and God; the total suppression of his Love nature. This had resulted in an enforced chastity, giving him power to avoid seduction - 'tis true - but likewise cutting him off from the possibility of redemption. For hear his words:

Awfulest strait! Irrepressible yearning woe! Terrible lust in me once rife, Which I had quenched with devilish strife; Mocks and laughs it at me, Thou devil's bride, through thee? Have a care!

In spite of further threats, we find Kundry still affirming that she will not conform to Klingsor's demands, yet, such is woman-kind, she quietly disappears to make ready for the reception and tempting of Parzival; who is at least a live and vigorous human being.

Klingsor has been watching Parzival's approach to his magic castle, armed - 'tis said - with the Sword of Innocence and protected by the Shield of Folly. Rather I should interpret this Sword as that of Reason, for Parzival has learned in his Folly to disarm and defeat the defenders of Klingsor's Castle with their own weapons.

There is no deeper wound than that inflicted by our own weapons turned against us; as Amfortas had found to his lasting pain and anguish.

The opportunities we have missed but had the power to take and might have taken, rankle more deeply than all the vain regrets for those things which were impossible of attainment.

But the mere possession of the most sacred weapon - as in the case of Klingsor and the Holy Spear - without further possibility of its right use, is bitterest of all.

And so we find, when Kundry has 'gone to work', Klingsor's Tower slowly sinks and disappears from sight. At the same time his "Garden of Desire" rises and his beautiful but illusory creations "The Flower Maidens" appear before our astonished eyes.

Parzival, whose desires have as yet given no indication of their presence, has by this time arrived at the wall of the garden. What he beholds is but subsidiary to his main Purpose to retrieve the Holy Spear, yet he, too, stands amazed.

This may be deemed as Parzival's introduction to "The Hall of Learning" as it is called by Madame Blavatsky in "The Voice of the Silence." Let us turn aside for a moment in order to obtain a clearer idea of just what that term implies. We read in Chapter I, Verses 22-29 as follows:

22. Three Halls, O weary Pilgrim, lead to the end of toils. Three halls, O conqueror of Mara, will bring thee through three states into the fourth, and thence into the Seven Worlds, the Worlds of Rest Eternal.

23. If thou would'st learn their names, then hearken, and remember. The name of the first hall is IGNORANCE - Avidya. It is the Hall in which thou saw'st the light, in which thou livest and shalt die.

Ignorance corresponds to Malkuth and Nepesh (the animal soul), Learning to Tiphareth and Ruach (the Mind), and Wisdom to Binah and Neshamah (the aspiration or Divine Mind). - Fra. O.M.

24. The name of Hall the second is the Hall of LEARNING. In it thy soul will find the blossoms of life, but under every flower is a serpent coiled.

25. The name of the third Hall is WISDOM, beyond which stretch the shoreless waters of AKSHARA, the indestructible Fount of Omniscience.

(Akshara is the same as the Great Sea of the Qabalah. It is also the CUP of the GRAIL, as WISDOM is the SPEAR.)

26. If thou wouldst cross the first Hall safely, let not thy mind mistake the fires of lust that burn therein for the sunlight of life.

27. If thou would'st cross the second safely, stop not the fragrance of its stupefying blossoms inhale. * * *

28. The WISE ONES tarry not in the pleasure grounds of the senses.

29. The WISE ONES heed not the sweet-tongued voices of illusion.

Enough has been quoted to show the extraordinary correspondences between the "Garden Scene" of the Drama of Parzival with both the Eastern Teachings and those of the Holy Qabalah. But this Drama is not subject to Time or Circumstance.

We left Parzival in a state of wonder upon the wall of Klingsor's Garden. We next find the "Flower Maidens" bemoaning the loss of their lovers - their pleasures - slain by Parzival upon his approach to the Castle and entry to the Garden.

Thye Flower Maidens are easily solaced, however, by the hope that here is a fresh pleasure, stronger and more potent than those lost to them. One that will more than take the place of all the others.

In this hope they are deceived for - as in real life - pleasures in time lose their hold (especially if abused) and though we may seek a stronger and more intense form of amusement, our power to enjoy may become dulled and lost to us.

The case in point is somewhat different, however, for the Flower Maidens find that the power to enjoy does not lie with them, for Parzival - with his One Purpose - is not to be turned aside for the sake of lesser pleasures.

Why should he, when by waiting he may gain All instead of a mere partial rapture? Has he not already experienced the Higher form of Ecstasy? The question now arises whether he had realised that this Higher Ecstasy with its Purity and STILLNESS is more to be esteemed than the APPARENT ACTIVITY of the lesser order.

In the Higher forms of Ecstasy characterized by this quality of STILLNESS, the ACTIVITY is in reality SO INTENSE that it appears to CEASE. But the resultant Rapture is in that case more refined and consequently more Powerful than in the Peace which passeth all understanding. Kundry may be said to have so far sought Rest below the Vibration of the RED RAY, while Parzival has found it beyond that of the ULTRA-VIOLET.

And so, when later, Kundry uses all her charms to tempt Parzival, she fails. Her embrace awakens the vibration of the RED RAY in the heart of Parzival and in this he recognizes, sympathetically, the cause of the wound of Amfortas and wherein the latter had failed. For Amfortas had been content to accept LESS than was his DUE, a vibration lower than the one to which his being was capable of responding.

Once the string of the Instrument or of the Bow has been slackened, its power is reduced; once the WILL has become the `will' it needs re-tuning to the Divine or Higher Vibration, but it cannot thus re-tune itself once self-will has usurped the place of SELF-WILL.

In that case the Holy Spear of Will and Wisdom has been replaced by the Sword of Reason. This Sword is both useful and necessary until man has obtained possession of the Holy Spear or become conscious of his true Purpose, (Just as Reason is necessary until we attain to Wisdom and Understanding whereby the Truth is directly perceived without the necessity of inference and deduction) but once the higher faculties have been acquired and the Higher Will recognized as the true guiding Power of our lives, our Purpose must be kept pure and unsullied.

This Mystery is made clear in Liber Al vel Legis:

"Let it be that state of manyhood bound and loathing. So with thy all; though hast no right but to do thy will. Do that, and no other shall say nay. For pure will, unassuaged of purpose, delivered from the lust of result, is every way perfect. The Perfect and the Perfect are one Perfect and not two; nay, are none!"

So we come to understand how the Perfect Cup and the Perfect Spear - Pure Understanding and Wisdom - are one; nay, are none since all `knowledge' is cancelled out in Perfect Ecstasy.

Parzival yields not to the glamour of time and circumstance for he seeks the Eternal Reality, the everpresent Here and Now. The chance of a brief reflection of ecstasy on the physical plane does not deter him from his Quest for that which is CONTINUOUS as the Body of Our Lady Nuit or the Stars of Heaven. But, meanwhile, since he has left behind him - in the Temple of the Grail - the true Chalice of Ecstasy, his first duty is to seek the Holy Spear, the means whereby alone it may be vivified and enlightened.

Under the influence of Kundry he obtains a glimpse of his true purpose, the mission of Redeemer. Having realized the cause of the wound of Amfortas he determines to seek and obtain the means whereby it may be cured. Nor is he to be turned aside from this deed of compassion for in vain does Kundry question:

And was it my kiss This great knowledge conveyed thee? If in my arms I might take thee, 'Twould then a god surely make thee. Redeem the world then, if 'tis thy aim: Stand as a god revealed; For this hour let me perish in flame, Leave aye the wound unhealed.

But Parzival is determined that he will first heal the wound of Amfortas - King of the Grail - and he offers Kundry redemption at the price of her showing him the way back to the Castle of the Grail.

This would perhaps have seemed the reasonable course for Kundry to pursue. But the Task of Parzival, by the proper performance of which he may become MASTER OF THE TEMPLE, is not thus easy of accomplishment.

He must, in fact, on his return to the Temple bring with him the NEOPHYTE in his hand. He must have proved his power to raise the Fallen Daughter - or Animal Soul - to the Throne of the Mother -Understanding. It is his task to lead Kundry to the Mountain of Salvation, not hers to show him the way.

Besides, he has not yet obtained the means of curing the wound of Amfortas. Mere compassion for his anguish, mere realization of the cause of the trouble is not enough. Had he returned at this juncture his mission would have been a failure.

But Kundry - womanlike - does not pursue the reasonable course, and in the end her intuition produces the finer flowering. Yet she is not conscious of this for the intuition is clouded in her mind by her emotional nature. She is aware that she has been flouted, that her charms have failed to seduce Parzival from the sacred mysteries, as she has seduced Amfortas. For Parzival has told her:

Eternally Should I be damned with thee, If for one hour I forget my holy mission, Within thine arm's embracing!

And this is no pleasant pill for any pretty woman to swallow.

Nor could her appeal to his pity (though in truth washed "By Pity 'lightened") turn him aside from his larger purpose; even when this appeal was coupled with the promise that he should straightway see the Path to the Grail if he lingered but an hour.

Desperate, Kundry cries:

"Begone, detestable wretch"

and calling upon Klingsor (the only Master Will she knows) to avenge her wrong, she at the same time curses Parzival and all the Paths wherein he might travel, should they lead away from her.

And here the intuition that she is really necessary to his Attainment actually brings about the next step towards that end, by strange means. Parzival needs above all to realize the Nature of his True Will. And Klingsor has at this moment appeared upon the Castle wall; the Damsels rushing out of the Castle hasten towards Kundry, while Klingsor - poising a lance - cries:

Halt there! I'll ban thee with befitting gear: The Fool shall perish by his Master's spear!

All else having failed, Klingsor make use of the Sacred Spear Itself. He hurls his WILL at Parzival, who, being perfectly receptive to the Higher Power (no matter what the agency used to bring it to him) receives the Spear, not in his heart, but in his hand. For - as in the case of the Higher WILL at the time of the opening of the 1001 petalled Lotus, the Real Flower of the Garden -it is seen gently floating above his head, within his reach and power to grasp.

And so Parzival grasps his True Purpose and brandishing the Holy Spear with a gesture of exalted rapture, he makes the Sign of the Cross therewith. Now the Sign of the Cross is symbolical of that "Cross of the Elements" from which the Creative Word issued at the birth of the dawning Universe.

A New Word is, as it were, uttered by Parzival and once again the Holy Spirit may be said to brood upon the Waters of Chaos. For at this moment, as with an earthquake, the Castle falls to ruins; the false Garden withers, and the damsels lie like shrivelled flowers strewn around on the ground. Kundry sinks down with a cry, and to her turns once more - from the summit of the ruined wall - the departing Parzival:

Thou knowst - Where only we shall meet again.

And, having uttered these prophetic words, he disappears among the shadows.

Point III
THE REDEMPTION OF THE REDEEMER

"Höchsten Heiles Wunder! Erlösung dem Erlöser!"

Before passing on to the final scenes of this Drama, it is necessary that we should know something of the Great Ceremony of Initiation into the Grade of Master of the Temple which Parzival was undergoing. This knowledge may best be obtained from the Records of the Great Brotherhood itself, and from the actual examples of those Who have undergone the Ordeals leading thereto.

The serious Student will be greatly interested in observing how closely some of the passages we have already quoted, and those we are about to quote, parallel the events in the Drama as compiled by Richard Wagner. But it must be remembered that Wagner himself received Instructions in the great Principles of the Holy Order from certain of the Secret Chiefs and this accounts for the great harmony between his Work and that of other members of the Great Brotherhood.

We find in Liber IV these words:

"The Master of the Temple has crossed the Abyss, has entered the Palace of the King's Daughter; he has only to utter one word, and all is dissolved. But, instead of that, he is found hidden in the earth, tending a garden. This mystery is all too complex to be elucidated in these fragments of impure thought; it is a suitable subject for meditation."

Parzival enters the Abyss when, casting aside every personal consideration and actuated by Pure Will delivered from the lust of result, he destroys Klingsor's Garden and Keep.

All that structure, built upon Reason, is shattered, and nothing but a rubbish-heap remains. For Parzival had discovered the Power of the Word whereby the Universe vanishes in Fire and

Flame. This may therefore be looked upon as the supreme Banishing Ritual.

But the process of Creation, Preservation and Destruction is continuous; things must be destroyed on order that they may be renewed. It is from the rubbish-heap of Chronozon (Klingsor) that one selects the materials for a god, or for a New Aeon. Understanding is the structuralization of knowledge, and implies coordination.

But, in the meanwhile Parzival must tend a Garden of his own, for, having looked upon the "Face of the Father" he has become NEMO - No-man. (It is interesting to note that Klingsor termed Kundry "Nameless woman", for she, too, must attain to Understanding in the end.)

A study of Liber CCCXVIII, 13th Aethyr, will give us a fuller comprehension of this Mystery. Therein we read:

"No man hath beheld the face of my Father. Therefore he that hath beheld it is called NEMO. And know thou that every man that is called NEMO hath a garden that he tendeth. And every garden that is and flourisheth hath been prepared from the desert by NEMO, watered with the waters that were called death. And I say unto him: To what end is the garden prepared? And he saith: First for the beauty and delight thereof; and next because it is written "And Tetragrammaton Elohim planted a garden eastward in Eden." And lastly, because though every flower bringeth forth a maiden, yet there is one flower that shall bring forth a man-child. And his name shall be called NEMO, when he beholdeth the face of my Father. And he that tendeth the garden seeketh not to single out the flower that shall be NEMO. He doeth naught but tend the garden. And I said: Pleasant indeed is the garden, and light is the toil of tending it, and great is the reward. And he said: Bethink thee that NEMO hath beheld the face of my Father. In his is only Peace. And I said: Are all gardens like unto this garden? And he waved his hand, and in the Aire across the valley appeared an island of coral, rosy, with green palms and fruit trees, in the midst of the bluest of the seas.

And he waved his hand again, and there appeared a valley shut in by mighty snow mountains, and in it were pleasant streams of water, rushing through, and broad rivers, and lakes covered with lilies. And he waved his hand again, and there was a vision, as it were an oasis in the desert. And again he waved his hand, and there was a dim country with grey rocks, and heather, and gorse, and bracken. * * * And he seems to read my thought, which is, that I should love to stay in this garden forever: for he sayeth to me: Come with me, and behold how NEMO tendeth his garden. So we enter the earth, and there is a veiled figure, in absolute darkness. Yet it is perfectly possible to see in it, so that the minutest details do not escape us. And upon the root of one flower he pours acid so that root writhes as if in a torture. And another he cuts, and the shriek is like the shriek of a mandrake, torn up by the roots. And another he chars with fire, and yet another he anoints with oil. And I said: Heavy is the labour, but great is the reward. And the young man answered me: He shall not see the reward; he tendeth the garden. And I said: What shall come unto him? And he said: This thou canst not know, nor is it revealed by the letters that are the totems of the stars, but only by the stars."

We find in the above an exact parallel to the case of Parzival, for he finds that "The Beatific Vision is no more, and the glory of the Most High is no more. There is no more knowledge. There is no more beauty. For this is the Palace of Understanding; and he is one with the Primeval things."

He must wander about in the earth, tending the ROOTS of the flowers; unconscious of the results of his labours, until the time is ripe for another to take his place.

The Third Act opens in the Grail's Domain. We perceive a pleasant spring landscape and flowery meadows towards the back. In the foreground is a wood which extends away towards the right, and a spring of clear water. Opposite, and higher up, is a narrow hermitage built against a rock. It is Daybreak.

All this brilliant spring scenery symbolises some of the work of Parzival who has laboured in darkness for many years. But the Night is nearly passed.

Gurnemanz, now old and in the garment of a simple hermit, yet still protected by the Mantle of the Grail, is now discovered. He hears a low moaning which he recognizes as that of Kundry, who- half dead, but now faithful in service - has found her way back to the Mountain of Salvation. Intuitively she had been led to keep her tryst with Parzival whose last words to her had been:

Thou knowest, where only we shall meet again.

She is discovered by Gurnemanz concealed in a small thicket near the stream. How long she has waited there, who can tell, but the thicket is now overgrown with thorns.

Upon spying her, Gurnemanz cries:

Up! - Kundry - Up! The winter's fled, and Spring is here! Awake, awake to the Spring!

The results of the unseen work of Parzival upon the "roots" of her being soon become apparent to Gurnemanz. Her first cry, on being aroused from her deadly stupor, is: Service!

But Gurnemanz - shaking his head - replies:

Now will thy work be light! We send no errands out long since: Simples and herbs Must ev'ry one find for himself: 'Tis learnt in the woods from the beasts.

But Kundry, having in the meanwhile looked about her, perceives the hermit's hut, and goes in. Gurnemanz, in surprise, remarks how different is her step, and thanks Heaven that he has been the means of reviving this "flower" that had formerly seemed so poisonous.

Kundry quietly returns with a water-pot which she takes to the spring, and while waiting for it to fill, she looks toward the wood and perceives a strange Knight approaching in the distance. She turns to Gurnemanz, who seeing the same figure, remarks:

Who comes toward the sanctified stream? In gloomy war apparel. None of our brethren is he.

For in his shroud of darkness Parzival - for it is he - is not recognized even by Gurnemanz, a Companion of the Grail. It is not surprising that during his wanderings those less enlightened should have failed to perceive his identity.

He slowly enters, clad from head to foot in pure black armour; carrying, upright, the Sacred Spear, equipped with sword and shield. He seems dreamy and vacillating, but seats himself on the little knoll beside the stream.

Gurnemanz, after observing him for some time, finding him silent, approaches somewhat, and remarks:

Greet thee, my friend! Art thou astray, and shall I direct thee?

In reply to which Parzival gently shakes his head, but remains silent. Further questioning only elicits from him the same silent response, for is it not written that UNDERSTANDING is pure Silence and Pure Darkness.

But the end of this period of silence and darkness is approaching. The NEMO stage of the "City of the Pyramids" soon gives place to another.

Parzival rises and thrusts his Spear upright in the ground, thus, as it were, linking Heaven and Earth. He then slowly divests himself of the black armour. First he lays down his Sword (The power of Reason and of analysis), and his Shield (The heavy Karma of the World - his Pantacle). Opening his Helmet (which, being but a symbol of the Cup, has kept him in a darkness) he removes it; thus allowing the Wine of Sunlight to descend upon his head.

He then kneels in silent prayer before the Spear, seeking conscious and enlightened union with the Will of the Universe. Hitherto he has been guided by that Will, but has remained the while unconscious of Its direction, he now seeks to participate more fully in the Great Purpose.

While thus engaged in holy meditation, he is recognised by both Gurnemanz and Kundry. They also realize that he has obtained possession of the Sacred Spear, so long lost to the Knights of the Grail. Kundry turns away her face, while Gurnemanz, in great emotion, cries:

Oh! - holiest day. To which my happy soul awakes!

Then, having arisen, Parzival recognises them in turn and greetings are exchanged. He can hardly believe that at last his path through error and suffering has led him once again to that holy spot. For all seems changed.

His one desire is to find Amfortas, whose wound had so long aroused his Compassion and Pity, and which he feels it to be his mission to heal. This may be accomplished by one means alone, the Sacred Spear by which the wound was made.

And all that while that Parzival - even with this high purpose in view - had consciously sought to return to The Mountain of Salvation, the path thereto had been denied him and he had wandered at random, as if:

Driven ever by a curse: Countless distresses Battles and conflicts Drove me far from the pathway; Well though I knew it, methought.

For the Road to Ecstasy is one above thought, and when Ecstasy returns it is as a Grace rather than as the result of our conscious efforts. Yet it is the reward of our "wanderings" if our Aspiration has been kept perfectly pure meanwhile.

The Sacred Spear - The True Will - must not be used save for the highest ends; and those ends do not become apparent to the conscious mind, till many a day after it has first been grasped and wielded to destroy illusion.

Parzival:

Then hopeless despair overtook me, To hold the holy Thing safely. In its behalf, in its safe warding I won from ev'ry weapon a wound; For 'twas forbidden That in battle I bore it: Undefiled E'er at my side I wore it, And now I home restore it. 'Tis this that gleaming hails thee here, - The Grail's most holy spear.

And then Parzival learns from Gurnemanz that he at last nears the end of his Quest, for he is already within the Grail's Domain. He learns, too, of the anguish that has been suffered by Amfortas during his absence, and how the Knights had been disbanded because Amfortas no longer dared to unveil the Holy Cup. How Titurel, Father and Founder of the Order, had died -

as other men - when he no longer received the Grail's enlivening beams.

So Parzival, in intense grief, bemoans his foolish wanderings that seem to have caused such disastrous results through his delay in returning to Monsalvat on his mission of mercy.

But things could have not been otherwise. We should remember how NEMO tended his garden and how some of the roots writhed in anguish under the acid or the knife, while others flourished by means of the oil.

Had his Understanding not been Pure Darkness, his conscious mind would never have allowed him to complete his Work. But such is the Mystery of Redemption that these things must be in order that the final outcome may be perfect.

Sorrow and suffering are great teachers, and the Masters, having no personal ends to accomplish, are often the Instruments whereby our Karma comes upon us. As pointed out in Liber IV.:

"The contemplation of the Universe must be at first almost pure anguish. It is this fact which is responsible for most of the speculation of philosophy. Medieval philosophers went hopelessly astray because of their theology necessitated the reference of all things to the standard of man's welfare. * * * The Ego-Idea must be ruthlessly rooted out before Understanding can be attained. There is an apparent contradiction between this attitude and that of the Master of the Temple. What can possibly be more selfish than this interpretation of everything as a dealing of God with the soul? But it is God who is all and not any part; and every "dealing" must thus be an expansion of the soul, a destruction of its separateness. Every ray of the sun expands the flower. The surface of the water in the Magick Cup is infinite; there is no point different from any other point. Thus, ultimately, as the wand (spear) is a binding and a limitation, so is the Cup an expansion - into the Infinite. And this is the danger of the Cup; it must necessarily be open to all, and yet if anything is put into it which is out of proportion, unbalanced, or impure, it takes hurt." But - "Ultimately the Magical Will so identifies itself with the man's whole being that it becomes unconscious, and is as constant a force as gravitation."

Thus had the Spear - The Magical Will - led Parzival back to the Grail.

But, after his long Quest, Parzival is weak and fainting, and this final temptation - the idea that after all he has FAILED in the Quest - causes him to sink down helplessly upon the grassy knoll.

Kundry has brought a basin of Water with which to sprinkle Parzival, but Gurnemanz, waving her off, says:

Not so! The holy fount itself Befitteth more our pilgrim's bath.

And so, by the side of the Holy Spring (The Waters of the Great Sea - AKSHARA) they remove the greaves from his legs (giving him further freedom of action) and bathe his feet (Symbol of Understanding). They then remove his corslet (thus disclosing his Heart) and sprinkle him with the holy water.

For there are Three that bear witness on Earth - The Water, the Blood and the Holy Ghost (the Dove) and he that overcometh shall partake of the Waters of Life freely.

Upon the contemplation of Kundry's self-imposed task of bathing the feet of Parzival, he asks gently but wearily:

"Shall I straight be guided unto Amfortas?"

To which question Gurnemanz, whilst busying himself, replies:

Most surely; there the Court our coming waits.

He explains further that even he has been summoned to this Reception since, upon the death of Titurel, the long neglected office of the uncovering of the Grail is, by the will of Amfortas, once more to be performed.

We should notice how, apparently by chance - for so seems the Design of the Universal Initiation of Humanity - all things have been prepared and are seen to lead up to the Crowning point of the Ceremony.

Meanwhile, Parzival sits wondering at the marked change in Kundry, at her now humble attitude, so different from her former perversity; while Gurnemanz performs a further office in the ceremony of Purification by sprinkling the head of Parzival with the water from the Holy Spring.

Purification being complete, is followed by Consecration, the second step towards Initiation. Kundry is seen to take a golden flask from her bosom and to pour some of its contents upon Parzival's feet. Taking the flask from her, Parzival then invites Gurnemanz to anoint his head with the same Holy Oil; his now clear vision causing him to remark:

"For I today as king shall be appointed."

He makes this statement, which is no less than a prophesy of his complete attainment, as simply and naturally as a child.

A few remarks should now be made on the nature of this Holy Oil and in regard to the source from whence it came. Liber IV will again supply the key, for therein we read:

"The Holy Oil is the Aspiration of the Magician, it is that which consecrates him to the performance of the Great Work. * * * It is not the will of the magician, the desire of the lower to reach the higher; but is that spark of the higher in the Magician which wishes to unite the lower with itself."

The Oil, in this instance performs a double purpose, for it represents both the awakening of the True Self of Kundry, and the desire for redemption. This Higher Self is represented by Parzival, and Kundry's Consecration of Parzival is the act which makes her redemption, by him, possible.

Again:

"This oil is compounded of four substances. The basis of all is the oil of the olive, The Olive is, traditionally, the gift of Minerva, the wisdom of God, the Logos. It is dissolved in three other oils; oil of myrrh, oil of cinnamon, oil of galangal. The Myrrh is attributed to Binah, the Great Mother, who is both the understanding of the Magician and that sorrow and compassion that results from the contemplation of the Universe. The Cinnamon represents Tiphareth, the Sun - the Son, in whom Glory and Suffering are identical. The Galangal represents both Kether and Malkuth, the First and the Last, the One and the

Many, since in this Oil they are One." "These oils taken together represent the whole Tree of Life. The ten Sephiroth are blended into the perfect gold." This will become clearer when the whole Drama has been treated from the Qabalistic viewpoint in the next Chapter. Again: "This perfect Oil is most penetrating and subtle. Gradually it will spread itself, a glistening film, over every object in the Temple."

In regard to this latter point we should observe what actually happens a little further on in the Drama, but first notice one further quotation which has a very direct bearing on the subject in hand.

"The phial which contains the Oil should be of clear rock crystal (Rock Crystal is attributed to Malkuth - the Fallen Daughter, but in this case the flask is of Gold which represents the Breast, Sun or Tiphareth Sphere of the Son or Higher Self whose influence has been felt by Kundry) and some magicians have fashioned it in the shape of the female breast, for that is the true nourishment of all that lives. For this reason also it has been made of mother-of-pearl and stoppered with a ruby."

In this connection we should note that Kundry produced the golden flask from her bosom, for every detail of this Drama is symbolical.

Next, Parzival very quietly scoops up some of the Holy Water from the Spring and sprinkles it upon Kundry's head while she kneels at his feet - saying:

I first fulfil my duty thus: - Be thou baptized, And trust in the Redeemer!

At which Kundry bows her head and appears to weep bitterly.

This is the first time that Kundry has been truly willing to receive the higher help. She has done much, according to her own notions of service, but now she is about to be led to Understand how best she may Serve; for true Mastery implies true Service.

We should notice, too, the effects of the Holy Oil on Parzival. He turns round and gazes with gentle rapture on the woods and meadows; which represent his Garden, as we explained before. Gradually, he realizes the results of the Work he had carried on in silence and darkness. His memory awakens and he murmurs:

How fair the fields and meadows seem today! Many a magic flower I've seen, Which sought to clasp me in its baneful twinings; But none I've seen so sweet as here, These tendrils bursting with blossom, Whose scent recalls my childhood's days, And speaks of loving trust to me.

Gurnemanz attempts to explain this, saying: "That is Good-Friday's spell, my lord!" Whereas Parzival, reminded of the darkness of his self-crucifixion and hardly yet realizing its full significance, replies:

"Alas, that day of agony! Now surely everything that thrives, That breathes and lives and lives again Should only mourn and sorrow?"

But Gurnemanz continues:

"Thou seest it is not so.

For:

"The sad repentant tears of sinners have here with holy rain besprinkled field and plain, and made them glow with beauty. All earthly creatures in delight at the Redeemer's trace so bright, uplift their prayers of duty. To see Him on the Cross they have no power; and so they smile upon redeemed man, who, feeling freed, with dread no more doth cower, through God's love-sacrifice made clean and pure. And now each meadow flower and blade perceives that mortal foot to-day it need not dread; for as the Lord in pity man did spare, and in His mercy for him bled, all men will keep with pious care, to-day a tender tread. So Trespass-pardoned Nature wakes now to her day of Innocence."

During this speech, Kundry has been watching Parzival with moist eyes and a look of beseeching, and he, now fully realizing the results of his work (for it is High Noon) remarks:

I saw my scornful mockers wither: Now look they for forgiveness hither? Like blessed sweet dew a tear from thee too floweth? Thou weepest - see! the landscape gloweth.

And he kisses her softly upon the brow. Here the "dew of pure love" begins its wondrous action which brings all to perfection. Of this it is written in Liber IV. "There is, however, a universal solvent and harmonizer, a certain dew which is so pure that a single drop of it cast into the water of the Cup will for the time being bring all perfection.

"This dew is called Love. Even in the case of human love, the whole Universe appears perfect to the man who is under its control, so it is, and much more, with the Divine Love of which it is now spoken.

"For human love is an excitement, and not a stilling of the mind; and as it is bound to the individual, only leads to greater trouble in the end.

"This Divine Love, on the contrary, is attached to no symbol. It abhors limitation, either in its intensity or in its scope."

Here we obtain the key to the errors of both Klingsor and Amfortas; together with the true solution of the problem, as obtained by Parzival. For this Love leads on to ECSTASY, as the drama itself now shows us.

It is MIDDAY, and just as the Sun is then at its height and full beauty, so we find that Parzival's travels have led him to complete the circle of his wanderings, and in another moment, The Mountain of Salvation, like a great Ruby Jewel set in a Golden Ring, will shine out once more. Meanwhile, Gurnemanz and Kundry are seen to cover Parzival with the Mantle of the Grail, and he, solemnly grasping the Holy Spear and with Kundry at his side, prepares to follow Gurnemanz.

Now, as if to prove out theory that Parzival had completed the Circle, we find the scenery once again automatically changing, but this time from right to left. It will be remembered that on the previous occasion, when for the first time Parzival entered the Temple of the Grail, this charge took place in the opposite direction. The passages through which they pass are similar, but as if reversed. And this time all three traverse them together as if to symbolise the Sacred Triad, the completion of which is about to take place.

As before, there are chimes of bells. (The aspirant will notice similar sounds when entering the Higher Consciousness. They are sometimes called "The Voice of the Nada.")

Once more Time and Space are One, and the Tableau of the Everpresent Here and Now appears.

Here we find Birth, Death, Life, Sorrow, Age and Youth mingled together in Harmony, Joy and Beauty. The vast Temple of the Holy Ghost - the length of which is from North to South, its breadth from East to West, and its height from Abyss to Abyss, yet which is also the BODY OF MAN - is open to our view.

There is but a faint light at first. The doors open on either side and Knights bring Titurel's corpse in a Coffin and Amfortas' wounded body on a litter. The bier is erected in the middle of the Hall, and behind it is the throne with canopy, where Amfortas is set down.

Then comes a train of Knights bearing the Holy Grail towards the sheltering Shrine, where it is placed as before.

Unaware of the approach of the Victorious Parzival, the Knights now murmur at the death of Titurel the honoured founder of the Order. For this death, Amfortas appears to have been at least partially responsible, having failed for so long a time in his office to unveil the Grail. Yet he, having lost the Sacred Spear - the Higher Will - entrusted to him by his Father, and having found the human will quite unable to take Its place, has in the meanwhile suffered awful tortures through this failure to fulfil his true Purpose.

The Knights, in despair, press towards Amfortas and demand that he - this once - unveil the shrine and do his office. Whereat, Amfortas in an ECSTASY OF FEAR, springs up and throws himself among the Knights - who draw back - while he cries:

No! - No more! - Ha! Already is death glooming round me, And shall I yet again return to life? Insanity! What one in life can yet stay me? Rather I bid ye slay me!

For such is the Ecstasy of the Touch of Death the Twin of Love.

(He tears open his dress.)

Behold me! - the open wound behold! Here is my poison - my streaming blood. Take up your weapons! Bury your sword-blades Deep - deep in me, to the hilts! Ye heroes, up! Kill both the sinner and all his pain: The Grail's delight will ye then regain!

But there is no DEATH in the Hall of Ecstasy. Birth, Life, Death are not successive but One, for Time and Space are One.

And so, at the moment of Amfortas' greatest agony Parzival, the Redeeming Power, enters unperceived and unexpected.

There is much truth in the old saying, "The unexpected is sure to happen" and this is more and more clearly realized as we tread the true Path. True Ecstasy comes at the moment when all seems lost, for the partial and transient must disappear and become lost, e'er the Real appears. "For to each individual thing, attainment means first and foremost the destruction of the individuality."

"Each of our ideas must be made to give up the self to the Beloved, so that we may eventually give up the Self to the Beloved in our turn." - Liber IV.

Suddenly the voice of Parzival is heard:

One weapon only serves: The one that struck Can staunch thy wounded side.

The countenance of Amfortas, upon his hearing these words, now displays HOLY RAPTURE. He totters in ecstasy, while Gurnemanz supports him tenderly.

Parzival:

Be whole, unsullied and absolved! For now I govern in thy place.

The True Will unhesitatingly takes its rightful place, and since that Will is one with THE WILL OF THE UNIVERSE, Amfortas without hesitation accepts it.

38

Parzival:

Oh blessed be thy sorrows, For Pity's potent might And Knowledge' purest Power They taught a timid Fool. The Holy Spear Once more behold in this.

And as all gaze in rapture on the Spear held aloft by Parzival, he continues, in inspiration, as he gazes at its Point:

O mighty miracle of bliss! This that through me thy wound restoreth. With holy blood behold it poureth, Which yearns to join the fountain glowing, Whose pure tide in the Grail is flowing! Hid be no more that shape divine; Uncover the Grail! Open the Shrine!

Thus, and not otherwise, came Parzival into his own. The Temple of the Chalice of Ecstasy is now, for him, The Palace of the King's Daughter. For thus is it written: "When these shall have destroyed the Universe, then mayest thou enter the Palace of the Queen, my Daughter." Then only shall we understand the nature of The Bride's Reception. For:

"The Spirit and the bride say, Come. And let him that heareth say, Come. And let him that is athirst come. And whosoever will, let him take of the water of life freely."

Thus, and thus alone; amid Radiant Light, the Glowing of the Chalice of Ecstasy, the Rising of Titurel from the Tomb, the Death struggle of Kundry, the Homage of the Redeemed, the Praise of the Knights of the Grail, and above all the Benediction of the Dove of the Holy Spirit; is the final Work accomplished -

THE REDEMPTION OF THE REDEEMER.

QABALISTIC CONCLUSION

Nothing now remains but for the scribe to bear witness to the strange Qabalistic "coincidences" connected with this Drama.

Was Wagner a great Qabalist? Were those from whom he obtained the sources of his information such? Who can tell?

Rather I would suggest that, being inspired, this Drama must of necessity conform to all truth, on all planes. For there are certain Numerical Emanations, called the Ten Sephiroth, and there are certain Vibrations of a numerical nature connected with Words.

It is not my intention to write a treatise on the Holy Qabalah (those who wish to study this interesting subject may do so in "Q.B.L. or The Bride's Reception"), nor to describe fully the "Tree of Life", nor the methods of drawing numerical meanings from words. The accompanying plate shows the structure of "The Tree of Life", and the Frontispiece indicates how the "Chalice of Ecstasy" may be drawn therefrom.

The Qabalistic teaching is that Malkuth - The Kingdom - The Animal Soul - THE FALLEN DAUGHTER must be RAISED through the Office of the SON - Tiphereth - The Sun - Harmony and Beauty, to the Throne of the MOTHER - Binah - Understanding - THE CUP, when she is again united to the FATHER - Chokmah - Wisdom - Will - THE SPEAR, thus absorbing all into THE CROWN - Kether - The Pure Light of the DOVE which descends upon their Union.

This is the Mystery of Redemption and of the Great Work, the Uniting of the Microcosm and the Macrocosm - Man with God.

The main Formula of the Great Work, that of the Rose and Cross, is symbolised in the Great Order as $5° = 6°$. This refers to the Microcosm and the Macrocosm as the Pentagram or Fivefold Star on Unconquered Will and the Hexagram or Six-fold Star. The Work is to discover their equivalence, and to unite them.

The first stage of this Union occurs in TIPHERETH, and is accompanied with the feeling of Ecstasy. This Sephira is that of the SUN, and is necessarily connected with the Solar Numbers of which 6, 66, and 666 are the Scale. This is the Sphere of the Crowned King - The Son who unites in himself both Glory and Suffering.

But since there has been, what we may term, a change of Office in the Great Hierarchy in this New Aeon, we find that the Number 418 which is the numeration of "ABRAHADABRA" the Word of the Aeon is also particularly attributed to this Sphere, since it represents perfectly the formula of 5°=6°. (See Sepher Sephiroth, Equinox Vol. I. Number VIII.)

Again 777 is a number representing alike "The Flaming Sword" and the Unity of all things including the World of Shells. In Greek Qabalah it corresponds to the word STAUROS - The Cross.

It is worthy of notice, and most careful consideration, therefore, that with slight adjustment of spelling, the Names of the principle characters in the Drama have an extraordinary significance.

TITUREL, Founder of the Grail Order, adds to 666.

MONSALVAT, the Mountain of Salvation, adds to 666.

GAMURET, the Father of Parzival, adds to 666.

AMFORTAS, with his Cross of Suffering, adds to 777.

KLINGSOR, who represents Choronzon (333) adds to 333.

GURNEMANZ, Conductor of the New King, adds to 418.

PARZIVAL, The Pure Fool, adds to 418.

KUNDRY and GUNDRYGGIA, alike add to 290.

In the above the Hebrew equivalents of the letters and the old spellings of the names are used. With small study of the Qabalistic System and the Grades of the Order based on the Tree of Life, the significance of the above will become more and more apparent to the Student. An extended treatise might be written on the subject, but that is not the intention of the author at this time.

Now, there are several spellings of the name Parzival; the one I have adopted being that of Wolfram von Eschenbach, from whom Wagner derived the Drama. The usual spelling - Parsifal - is interesting since it adds to 388, which, with the addition of 500 (Final Mem. The Water of the Great Sea of Understanding), becomes 888. By Greek Numeration 888 is the number of Jesus the Christ.

But there is another spelling, much more significant, and probably the oldest of them all. PARCHVAL, the numeration of which adds to 326.

It will have been noticed that the most important Points of the Drama are connected with THE CUP - Understanding - Binah the THIRD Sephira; The SPEAR - Will - Wisdom - Chokmah the SECOND Sephira, and THE HEART - The Castle of the Grail - Tiphereth the SIXTH Sephira. If we examine these Spheres on the Tree of Life we find they form a Descending Triad representing the Bowl of The Chalice of Ecstasy, the points of which are 326.

Now 326 is the Numeration of IHShVH - The Hebrew Jeheshuah - Jesus - The God- Man or Redeemer. This Word also symbolises the descent of "Shin" the letter of the Holy Spirit into the Four Lettered Word IHVH - Jehovah - The Ineffable Name and the Formula of the Four Elements. Thus PARChVAL symbolises the whole process perfectly; the Descent of Spirit into Matter and also of the Redemption.

It also shows the transition to the New Aeon, there being a connection between this old spelling and that of Parzival the formula of the present time. For the central letter of the word PARChVAL is "Ch" in Hebrew Cheth, which spelt in full is 418 the numeration of Parzival, and of the Word of the Aeon, his Magick Formula.

I need only add that The DOVE - Kether - The Crown - when shown above the bowl of the CHALICE (in its natural position on The Tree of Life) together with Yesod - the Foundation and Malkuth - The Kingdom, as the stem and base of the Cup; completes the Qabalistic Design. This arrangement clearly shows how the Chalice is one with the Tree of Life and filled by the Holy Spirit.

The numerical proof is not, however, quite complete - indeed it could never be completed - but let me draw your attention to the word Grail. The old spelling is GRAL and here we find G - the letter of The Moon - and R - the letter of the Sun, coupled with AL, the Great Name of God.

Turning once more to our Qabalistic Design of the Cup drawn on the Tree of Life, let us examine the Numbers of the Sephiroth involved. We shall indeed discover the "Chalice of Ecstasy" for we obtain $1 + 2 + 3 + 6 + 9 + 10 = 31$, which is the numeration of both AL and LA - God and Not- Key to the Mysteries both of the Old Aeon and the New and when properly understood the Final Formula of

ECSTASY.

-oOo-